Gregory Fuller

Tom's adventures in Catland

and other stories

Ernst Klett Verlag
Stuttgart · Leipzig

Als Ergänzung zu dieser Lektüre bieten wir **Downloadmaterialien** für Lehrkräfte für den Unterrichtseinsatz bzw. für die Unterrichtsvorbereitung an. Bitte geben Sie unter www.klett.de diesen Online-Link in das Suchfeld ein:

547070-0001

Textquelle:
S. 27: *Mice* by Rose Fyleman is reproduced by permission of The Society of Authors.

1. Auflage 1 10 9 8 7 6 | 2020 19 18 17 16

Redaktion: Virginia Maier

Satz und Gestaltung: Jacqueline Köhler
Illustrationen: David Norman, Meerbusch
Druck: AZ Druck und Datentechnik GmbH, Kempten

Printed in Germany.
ISBN 978-3-12-547070-5

9 783125 470705

Contents

Tom and the ghost

Pre-reading:

1. What do you know about ghosts? Make a list.
2. What do you think: Are there ghosts or not?

Start like this:
I think there are/aren't ghosts because …

Everything is quiet at Thomas Tallis School in Greenwich. Everything? Yes! But not *everybody*. It is night and Tom Tiny, the school mouse, is looking for food. Thomas Tallis is a great place for food. The pupils leave chocolate and fruit and crisps and sandwiches in the cafeteria and in the classrooms.

But tonight Tom looks and looks. He can't find anything.

Where is the good food? Tom thinks. Hm. It isn't here.

He looks in the cafeteria. It is clean.

What can he do?

Oh! Tom thinks. It was that idiot, Mr Newman, the caretaker! Everything is so clean.

"This is really bad!" Tom shouts.

Suddenly he hears a funny noise. He wants to run away.

"What is bad, little man?" a voice says.

"Help! A voice!" Tom shouts. "Where are you?"

"Oh," says the voice. "Sorry. Here I am!"

A big white man is standing there.

"Ah!" Tom shouts. "I can see through you! Oh no, a ghost! Help!"

---

8 **not … anything** ['eniθiŋ] *hier:* nichts • 12 **was** [wəz] war • 15 **noise** [nɔɪz] Geräusch

STOP Who do you think the ghost is?

Tom is scared and starts to run away.

"Wait!" The white ghost is behind him.

Tom stops. He turns and looks at the ghost.

"Are you … are you a *nice* ghost?" asks Tom.

"Oh, yes, my friend, I am," the ghost answers.

"Hm," says Tom, "I was a bit scared there. But only a bit. Uh … are you sure you are a nice ghost?"

The ghost smiles.

"Of course I am a nice ghost, Mr Mouse. And now: Guess who I am. This is my home."

"Uh … are you the ghost of a headteacher?"

The ghost laughs.

"Look at me, Mr Mouse. Look."

Tom looks at him. His clothes are very old.

"Mr Ghost, I don't know. Who are you?"

The ghost says, "I am Thomas Tallis."

7 **was** [wəz] war • 8 **sure** [ʃʊə] sicher

"Oh – Thomas Tallis? I know you! The great composer and organist, from, uh, 1550? You are famous, Mr Tallis! This school has got your name."

Suddenly the ghost looks sad. He sits down. Then he says: "But you don't know my music, do you?"

Tom sits down next to the ghost.

"No, Mr Tallis, I don't know your music. Sorry."

"Of course you don't. That's my problem. They don't play my music today. I must walk through Thomas Tallis School – *my* school – every night until …"

"Until …?" Tom asks.

"… until they play my music here at Thomas Tallis. Then I can rest."

1 composer [kəm'pəʊzə] Komponist • **2 organist** ['ɔːgənɪst] Organist • **4 sad** [sæd] traurig • **4 (to) sit down** [sɪt 'daʊn] sich hinsetzen • **10 until** [ʌn'tɪl] bis • **13 (to) rest** [rest] ruhen, sich ausruhen

Tom wants to help the sad ghost.

"A – ha. Your music. They must play it here. Mr Tallis, let me think about that. Can we meet here in the cafeteria tomorrow night?"

"Of course, my friend, of course. I've got lots and lots and lots of time. Goodbye."

"Goodbye, Mr Tallis."

Tom goes back to his home. He is tired, but he can't sleep. He does not go to bed. He sits on his sofa and thinks and thinks. Then, in the morning, suddenly Tom has got an idea. He is happy.

Wow! Now the ghost can be happy, too, Tom thinks.

It is quiet, very quiet again the next night. Tom is waiting for the ghost of Thomas Tallis in the cafeteria. Tom is a bit scared, but he is excited, too.

"Mr Ghost? Mr Tallis?" Tom asks.

Suddenly the white ghost is there.

"Oh, hello, Mr Tallis," Tom says and smiles.

"Hello, Mr Mouse, Mr – ?"

"Tiny, I'm Tom Tiny."

The ghost laughs: "Mr Tiny, very nice."

"I can help you, Mr Tallis. I've got an idea. But can you help *me*?"

"And what is *your* problem, Mr Tiny?"

"I'm hungry, Mr Tallis, very hungry. Mr Newman, the school caretaker, cleans everything every day, and I can't find the cheese anywhere!"

4 **tomorrow** [tə'mɒrəʊ] morgen • 27 **not ... anywhere** [nɒt...'enɪweə] nirgendwo

The ghost laughs. Then he says, "I can help you, Mr Tiny. And what is your plan for me?"

Tom tells his idea to the ghost. The ghost laughs again. He really likes Tom.

"You are small, Mr Tiny, but you are smart. Let's start!"

The ghost of Thomas Tallis opens the cupboard door in the cafeteria. He does not need a key. He shows Tom how he can open the cupboard without a key.

The cupboard has got lots of cheese. Tom eats and eats. He is very happy.

The next morning Mrs Carter's pupils go into their classroom. Terry sits down at his place. What does he see?

5 **smart** [smɑ:t] klug

"Hey, what's this?" he asks his friend Lisa.

There are lots of pages of music on his desk – music by Thomas Tallis. Terry can read music. He likes it. He wants to play the music with his band, the Tom-Toms. But the music is not easy, and it is not fast. This is very new music for Terry. He does not know what to do. Then he has got an idea. After the lesson he asks Lisa, "Hey, Lisa. Your mum has got a jazz café ..."

"Yes, that's right, Terry."

"Can I go and talk to her today after school?"

"Huh? My mum? But why?"

"Maybe she can help me with this old music ... and make it exciting for the Tom-Toms. Then we can play it. The boys in the band like fast music."

"Oh, OK. Good idea. My mum is great with music. She can help you."

After school Lisa and Terry go to Sue Taylor's jazz café. Barker is there, too. He is happy and runs to Lisa and Terry and barks.

"Watch out, Barker!" Terry says. "I've got very old music here."

Then he shows the music to Lisa's mum.

"Wow, Terry! This is great!" she says. "Terry, this is very, very interesting, and very old. Look – oh no! Look here – it says it is music by Thomas Tallis, the composer. Oh, Terry, you must give these pages of music to the Greenwich library. Wow!"

"OK," says Terry, "they can have the music, Mrs Taylor. But first the Tom-Toms want to play the music, but it isn't very fast. Can you help me with the music?"

"Of course, Terry. This is exciting! I can make it fast like real rock music. Is that OK?"

"Oh, yes, Mrs Taylor. Great! Thank you very much."

A few weeks later, Mrs Taylor has got the music for Terry and the Tom-Toms. Terry is very excited. The Tom-Toms

2 music [ˈmjuːzɪk] *hier:* Musiknoten • **2 by** [baɪ] von play Thomas Tallis's new but old rock music in Terry's shed. They like it very much, and Lisa thinks it is great.

In June they play the music at a big Thomas Tallis school concert in the Thomas Tallis Eatery. It is night, and Mrs Taylor and Lisa are there. And the ghost of Thomas Tallis is there, too – but only Tom can see him! Tom is in the cupboard. He listens to the music and sees the ghost of Thomas Tallis. The ghost is smiling: Now he can rest.

Everybody likes the interesting music, and Terry says "Thank you!" to Mrs Taylor. Everybody is happy, and Tom has got lots of cheese.

"But who put the music on my desk?" Terry wants to know.

In the cupboard, Tom hears Terry's question, and smiles.

The ghost of Thomas Tallis thinks: Tom is the best mouse in the world!

4 **concert** [ˈkɒnsət] Konzert • 12 **put** [pʊt] hat … hingelegt

Goodbye, Elephant!

Pre-reading:

Think about this: What do mice love? The story is about this!

Thomas Tallis School is a great place for a mouse. Every day Tom has got a lot to eat. He can open the cupboard without a key now, but there is too much cheese in the cafeteria cupboard for one little mouse, and there are chocolate and crisps there, too. So Tom writes an e-mail to his family:

Dear Mum and Dad,

Come to my home sweet home at Thomas Tallis now. There is too much food here. Bring Tim and Tess and Grandma Tilly and Grandad Thomas, too!

CU soon, Tom

The next day, the Tiny family is at Thomas Tallis. Everybody is happy to see Tom, and Tom is very excited, too.

"Uh, Tom," says Tim. "I'm hungry. Where's the food?"

Tom laughs and says, "Sorry, Tim. We must wait for the night. There are too many children here in the morning and in the afternoon. At night I can open the cupboard door in the school cafeteria. It is full of chocolate, crisps and cheese!"

"Chocolate. Crisps! And cheese!!" everybody shouts.

---

elephant ['elɪfənt] Elefant

Soon it is night. Seven Tiny mice go to the cafeteria. They go straight to the cupboard. But suddenly there is a big cat in the cafeteria in front of the cupboard.

"Help!" Tim shouts. "Mum!" The mice are very scared and run away.

Mr Newman, the caretaker, has got a new cat, a very, very big cat. His name is Elephant.

Back in Tom's home, the Tinys do not know what to do. A big cat is scary for seven little mice.

"Let's think a minute," Tom says. "There is one silly cat, and we are seven smart mice."

The Tinys sit and think.

STOP What would *you* do to get into the cupboard?

11 **smart** [smɑːt] klug

Then Tom says, "How about a joke? Seven mice can bark like a dog, can't they?"

Everybody laughs.

The next night, the Tinys go back to the cafeteria and hide behind a chair. Elephant is waiting at the cupboard.

Tom says, "One, two, three: bark!" And the Tinys bark like Barker, the dog.

"Aaaaah! A dog! Meow!" shouts the cat and runs away.

Tom and his family laugh, and they eat lots of chocolate, crisps and cheese.

But the next morning Mr Newman is not happy.

"Bad cat!" he says. "Back to the cafeteria tonight, Elephant!"

"Meow?" says Elephant.

"Catch those mice tonight, silly cat, or back to the pet shop with you, Elephant! Do you understand?"

"Me – oow," says Elephant.

But Tom has got a new plan. –

It is night at Thomas Tallis. Elephant is waiting for the mice in the school cafeteria.

"We've got a nice surprise for that big cat," Tom says.

The Tinys do not go to the cupboard.

It is twelve o'clock. It is one o'clock. It is two o'clock. It is three o'clock in the morning. The mice can wait.

At four o'clock in the morning Elephant is very tired. He falls asleep

The mice go behind the big cat and tie ten tins to Elephant's tail. Then they hide. Tom throws an old pencil at the tins. There is a terrible noise.

"Ah! Ah! Meow!" shouts the cat, and runs away. And he runs and runs and runs with the loud tins on his tail. He runs through Greenwich and he runs through London to Dog Street. There are a lot of dogs there, and they bark at

5 **(to) hide** [haɪd] verstecken • 15 **(to) catch** [kætʃ] fangen • 27 **(to) tie ten tins to** [taɪ ten ˈtɪns tə] zehn Dosen binden an • 29 **terrible noise** [ˈterɪbl nɔɪz] schrecklicher Lärm

him and the loud tins, and it is scary for Elephant. So he runs and runs and he swims to France.

The Tiny mice are very happy, and Tom opens the cupboard door for them.

"Welcome to my cupboard," he says.

"Chocolate. Crisps! And cheese!!" Tim and Tess shout.

"That's my son, Tom," Tamara Tiny laughs. "The best mouse in the world!"

Tom's adventures in Catland

Pre-reading:

1. What do you think "Catland" is?
2. Guess: Why does Tom go to Catland?

"Oh, no!" Tom shouts.

"Have you got a problem?" the man at the newsagent asks.

Tom is reading the newspaper, the *Greenwich Mouse Ear.*

"*We've* got a problem, Ben. Listen: 'The bad cats of Catland in south London have kidnapped Susie Sweet today. Nobody can find her. So she can't sing and dance and act at the Festival. Goodbye, Susie!'"

Tom goes home. He wants to cry. But then he thinks: No! Susie Sweet is a great mouse. I must go and find her in Catland!

Susie Sweet is a famous mouse in Greenwich. Everybody knows her. Every year at the Great Greenwich Mouse Festival, she sings super songs: *Sugar Mouse, I am your sugar mouse* and *Cheese around the clock* and *I wanna hold your ears.*

STOP Ask your teacher or your parents:
What are the *real* names of these songs?

Tom likes her great voice.

Susie Sweet acts in mouse plays. She often plays the role of Mousette in *Romeo and Mousette.* Everybody likes that, too.

---

7 **have kidnapped** [həv ˈkɪdnæpt] haben entführt • 8 **nobody** [ˈnəʊbədi] niemand • 16 **(to) cry** [kraɪ] weinen • 17 **I wanna hold your ears** [aɪ ˌwɒnə həʊld jər‿ˈeəz] *(umgangssprachlich)* Ich will deine Ohren halten

But when she dances the Mouse-Mouse, every mouse in London is there! Tom sees her every year. He *loves* it when she dances the exciting Mouse-Mouse. It is beautiful.

"More! More!" he shouts, and hundreds and hundreds of mice shout, "More, Susie! More!"

It is night. Tom starts to walk to Catland in south London. But then he stops. He thinks: Wait, Tom, old boy. Catland is far. And I can't fight those bad cats alone. I need a friend. A big friend. Who is big? Who can help me? ... Hm. ... Yes, Barker, the dog! He's a nice dog. He can help me.

Tom goes to Lisa's house where Barker lives. But what is that? He hears strange sounds.

"Woof – oo – oo – oo!"

1 **when** [wen] wenn • 8 **far** [fɑː] weit • 12 **strange** [streɪndʒ] merkwürdig

Then Tom sees Barker. He is in the dog house in the garden. He is not happy. He is chained to the dog house.

"Hi, Barker!" Tom says. "What is this?"

"Woof – oh – oo – oo, hi, Tom. I caught a cat today and Lisa was angry and chained me to the dog house for the night. And no food tonight! Woof – oh! I'm very hungry."

"Hm," says Tom. "I can help you, old boy. But can you help me tonight, too?"

"Get the key and my food, and I'm your dog tonight!" Barker smiles.

"OK, Barker. Tell me where the key is, and I can find the dog food in the kitchen."

Barker tells him.

"Wait five minutes, Barker."

2 is chained to [ɪz ˈtʃeɪnd tə] ist angekettet an • **4 caught** [kɔːt] fing • **5 was** [wəz] war

Tom runs into the house. Then he goes into Lisa's bedroom. He is very quiet. He sees the key on her table and takes the key.

After that he goes to the kitchen. There is a bowl of dog food there. Ten minutes later, Tom is back with the key and the big bowl of dog food.

"Woof! Woof! Tom! Great mouse!"

Tom unlocks the chain. After his late dinner, Barker says, "Ah! That's better! Woof! Now I'm a real dog again. And I'm a free dog, too! Thank you, Tom. Now, what's your problem?"

Tom tells him about Susie Sweet and the bad cats from Catland.

Barker laughs: "I love cats!"

"Huh?" asks Tom.

STOP Does Barker *really* love cats?

"I love to *chase* them!" says Barker. Now Tom laughs, too.

"Let's go, Tom. Catland, here we come! Climb up on my back, my friend."

Barker runs and runs through London. Soon Barker and Tom are in Catland.

"Let's stop here, Barker, and listen," Tom says. "Maybe we can hear Susie's voice."

"OK, Tom."

They listen and listen. Everything is quiet in Catland. Tom climbs down from Barker and listens again.

Suddenly a Catland guard cat jumps at Tom. Tom jumps up at Barker, Barker starts to bark – and Tom jumps into Barker's mouth!

8 **Tom unlocks the chain.** [tɒm ʌn'lɒks ðə 'tʃeɪn] Tom schließt die Kette auf. • 20 **Climb up on my back.** ['klaɪm ʌp ɒn maɪ 'bæk] Steig hinauf auf meinen Rücken. • 28 **guard** [gɑ:d] Wächter • 28 **(to) jump at** ['dʒʌmp ət] springen nach • 30 **mouth** [maʊθ] Mund

"Don't swallow!!" Tom shouts.

"Mm-I-m don't-m eat-m mice-m," Barker tries to say, with Tom in his mouth.

The cat runs away. Barker opens his mouth, and Tom is free.

"Oh – oh – boy!" Tom says.

"Dog food is better," Barker says, and the two friends laugh.

"Hey, Barker, look at this. The cat guard has got a spear. Maybe I can use it later."

"Good idea, Tom," Barker answers. "But now: Where's your mouse friend?"

"We must find another cat and ask it," says Tom.

"Quiet now," Barker answers. "We haven't got very many friends in Catland."

1 **(to) swallow** ['swɒləʊ] schlucken • 9 **spear** [spɪə] Speer

They walk through the quiet streets of Catland. No cats. It is very late. Then they see an old cat, and Barker stops next to it and says: "Hello, hello, hello, Mrs Cat. Woof!"

This is very scary for the old cat.

"P – p – please don't eat me! Meow!" she says, and falls over.

"Oops! Hello? Hello, Mrs Cat?" Tom asks.

But the old cat can't say a word. She is too scared.

"Oh, Barker. The poor old cat. We're too scary for an old cat. We must find a young cat."

"OK, Tom."

The cat guard has told the other cat guards about Tom and Barker. Barker and Tom do not know this. The cat guards are waiting for them behind a big tree.

Barker stops and says to Tom, "Quiet! I smell cats here. Ah – there they are – behind that tree. OK, cats, you pigs! Tom, sit on me, take the spear, and together we can be two scary animals!"

Tom sits on Barker with the big spear. Barker runs to the tree. This is a surprise for the cats.

"Hey, cats! Woof! Woof!"

"Meow! Help! Meow!" the cats shout. "Help! A big dog – and he's got a spear! Ow, ow!"

"Bad cats," Tom shouts, and he repeats Barker's words: "Woof! Woof!"

The cats run away. Tom and Barker laugh.

"Oh, Barker, you're great! Thank you. This is fun."

"Tom, my little friend, thank *you* for this great fun. But this doesn't help us to find your friend, Susie. Hm. What can we do?"

Tom sits and thinks. Then he smiles.

"I've got it, Barker. Let's look for a cat disco. There are always lots of young cats there. They're there every night. They know the exciting things here in Catland, and they must tell us everything."

9 **poor** [pʊə] arm • 12 **has told** [həz ˈtəʊld] hat erzählt • 15 **(to) smell** [smel] riechen • 34 **things** [θɪŋz] Dinge

"They *must*," Barker repeats.

The two friends look for a disco. They walk and walk through the night. Finally they see a few cool young cats. They are standing and talking. But when they see Barker and Tom, they run away.

"Silly cats," Barker says.

Tom and Barker go into the disco, the *Very cool cat*. The cats are dancing and the music is very loud. When the cats see Barker, the music stops. The cats want to leave, but Barker says, "Woof! I'm a nice dog, but I like to eat cats! So tell me where Susie Sweet, the mouse, is or I'll eat every cat in this disco!"

Then one cat says,"Please, Mr Dog, I can tell you. There is a big birthday party tonight for the Big White Cat, our king. There is a mouse there, but I don't know her name. She must sing and dance for the Big White Cat. P – p – please don't eat us, big dog!"

Tom and Barker smile.

"Thank you, cat," Barker says, "and where's the party?"

"G – g – go left down Cat Street, turn right into Big Cat Road, cross Cat Bridge at the river and the birthday party is in Catland Park, Mr Dog."

"Thank you again, cat."

"P – p – please don't eat us, Mr Dog!"

Barker smiles. "You're lucky! I'm not hungry now, cats."

Barker and Tom leave, they turn left into Cat Street, then they turn right into Big Cat Road and cross Cat Bridge.

"Stop, Barker," Tom says. "I can hear the music now. Oh! And I can hear Susie's great voice. Listen. She's singing *Yesterday, all the cats were, oh, so far away.*"

Barker smiles, "We can save her, Tom. But first let's stop and think."

Tom sits next to his friend. Then he says, "I've got it, Barker. There will be lots of cats at the Big White Cat's

---

11 **I'll (= I will)** [aɪl] ich werde • 15 **king** [kɪŋ] König • 30 **were, oh, so far away** [wɜː əʊ sə fɑː əˈweɪ] waren, ach, so weit weg • 31 **(to) save** [seɪv] retten • 34 **there will be** [ðeə wəl bi] es werden … sein

birthday party. We can't fight every cat. But listen to this …" and he tells his plan to Barker.

"Woof! Woof!" Barker says. "That's easy."

Tom sits on Barker and takes the spear. Barker goes into the park. He waits behind a big tree. Now Tom and Barker can see the cats. There are hundreds of cats. The Big White Cat is sitting on his throne. He looks happy. He is watching Susie Sweet! She doesn't look happy, but she is singing a song for him and for the cats.

"Let's go, Tom!" Barker shouts.

Then he runs to the stage.

"Woof! Woof! Woof!" Barker barks.

7 throne [θrəʊn] Thron • **11 stage** [steɪdʒ] Bühne

The music stops. It is a bad surprise for the cats – and a nice surprise for Susie Sweet! Some cats run away. The cats are scared, and the Big White Cat gets up and wants to run away, too. But it is too late. Suddenly Barker and Tom are on the stage next to the Big White Cat.

"Stop, King Cat!" Tom shouts.

He puts the point of his spear next to the Big White Cat's head.

"Your life, White Cat, or Susie Sweet!" Tom shouts.

The Big White Cat is very, very scared and he can't say a word. And the other cats can't speak. Everybody is quiet.

Suddenly Susie Sweet says, "Oh! Is that you, Tom? Yes! Oh, Tom!"

"Yes, Susie, it's me, Tom Tiny, and this is my friend, Barker."

"Hello, Susie," Barker says. "Well, big cat, your life or Susie. Speak!" he says to the Big White Cat.

The Big White Cat can talk again. "Mm – mm – Mr Dog, my life, please, please, please. You can take the little mouse, Mr Dog. Just – just go away, Mr Dog. Please!"

STOP What do *you* think of the Big White Cat?

"OK, cat. Susie, you can sit next to Tom. Let's go."

Susie and Tom are sitting on Barker. The cats are still quiet and scared. Barker walks away.

Soon the friends are not in Catland. They are going through south London. Barker is taking Susie and Tom back to Greenwich.

"Oh, Tom," Susie Sweet says and smiles at him. "Thank you very much! And thank you, too, Barker."

"You're welcome, Susie."

"You saved my life, you two," Susie smiles. "You're great, Tom. You're the best mouse in the world!"

---

7 point [pɔɪnt] Spitze • **31 You saved my life.** [jʊ ˌseɪvd maɪ ˈlaɪf] Du hast/Ihr habt mir das Leben gerettet.

Fun exercises for "Tom and the ghost"

1 Mouse jokes

Do you know any mouse jokes? Tell them to your partner.

Nine pieces of cheese

Mouse teacher: First I give you three pieces of cheese and then I give you five pieces of cheese. How many pieces of cheese have you got?

Tom: I've got nine pieces of cheese.

Mouse teacher: Nine?

Tom: Yes, that's right. I've got one piece of cheese at home!

Nine apples

Mouse teacher: I've got four apples in one hand and five apples in the other hand. What have I got?

Tom: Big hands.

2 A crossword puzzle

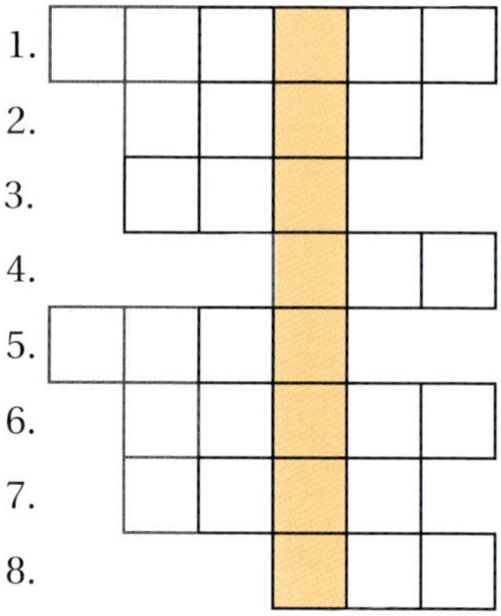

Across:

1. You can eat c … s.
2. You do this with music. You … it.
3. When he sees the ghost, Tom wants to do this.
4. Not night.
5. Tom says to the ghost: "I kn… you!"
6. You talk with your v…
7. The ghost is … to Tom.
8. Now Tom … got a lot of cheese.

Down: You often eat this at school: _ _ _ _ _ _ _ _

3 Put the sentences in the right order.

☐ A. Tom looks at him. His clothes are very old. *C*
[1] B. Everything is quiet at Thomas Tallis School in Greenwich. *N*
☐ C. "It was that idiot, Mr Newman, again!" *I*
☐ D. Tom is the best mouse in the world! *T*
☐ E. Now the ghost can be happy, too, Tom thinks. *E*
☐ F. "You are small, Mr Tiny, but you are smart." *H*
☐ G. This is very new music for Terry. *O*
☐ H. "Hey, Lisa. Your mum has got a jazz café ..." *S*

Start like this: Sentence B is number 1.

Now put the letters in the right order. What do they spell?

N __ __ __ *G* __ __ __ __
1 2 3 4 5 6 7 8

4 Post-reading

1. Who is Thomas Tallis?
2. a) Why must the ghost of Thomas Tallis walk through the school at night?
   b) Do you know any other stories like this?
3. What do you think: Who put the music on Terry's desk?

5 Four mouse brothers

Four mouse brothers live in Greenwich. The brothers' names are Tony, Peter, James and Ben Mouse. They all have got different jobs. One of them is a teacher, one is a taxi driver, one is a farmer and one is a bus driver.

Which mouse does which job? This can help you:

- The taxi driver often visits Tony at the weekends.
- Ben often goes to the cinema with the bus driver.
- Peter and Ben sometimes play cards with the taxi driver and the farmer.

Fun exercises for "Goodbye, Elephant!"

1 First letter – last letter

Play a word game with the words in this story.

mice
l
e
p
h
a
n
tonight …

You and your partner have got five minutes. Who wins?

2 Spot the difference

3 Mice *by Rose Fyleman*

I think mice
Are rather nice.
Their tails are long,
Their faces small,
They haven't any
Chins at all,
Their ears are pink,
Their teeth are white,
They run about
The house at night.
They nibble things
They shouldn't touch
And no one seems
To like them much.
But I think mice
Are nice.

a) *Look up the words you do not know in a dictionary.*
b) *Do* you *like mice? Why or why not?*

4 Post-reading

1. Tom has got two ideas to scare the cats. What are they?
2. Think about the story: Are cats *really* silly like this?

5 Droodles[1]

a) *What are they doing?* b) *Draw* your *droodles.*

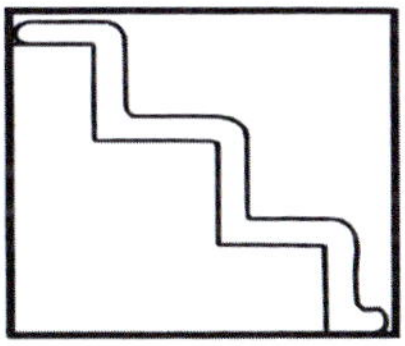

A snake is ...

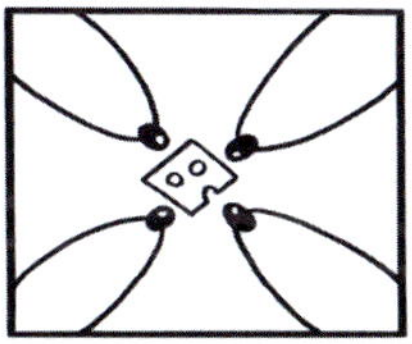

Four mice are ...

A Mexican is ...

1 **droodle** ['dru:dl] Drudel *(Bilderrätsel)*

Fun exercises for "Tom's adventures in Catland"

1 How many?

Look at the picture and say how many things you can see in Catland. Start like this:

I can see ... There are ... On the left/right there are ...

2 One letter

The first pupil goes to the board and writes a letter on it – the first letter of a word. The next pupil writes another letter after it, then the next pupil ...

Example:
C – H – E – ... can be *cheese* or *check-in* or *check-out*.

You must write the letter of a real word, or you are 'out'!

3 One word

In this game you try to tell a story. But one person can say only one word. Here is an example:

4 Post-reading

1. Why are the cats scared of Barker?
2. Why do Tom and Barker look for a cat disco?
3. What is a bad surprise for the cats at the birthday party?
4. Tom helps Barker and Barker helps Tom.
   a) Is this a good idea?
   b) Do you know any good examples of when people help other people?

5 Tom's game

Tom likes to play this game at birthday parties.
Look at this picture for a minute. Then close your reader and write down what you can remember.

Solutions

Tom and the ghost

Exercise 2:
Across: 1. crisps 2. play 3. run 4. day 5. know 6. voice 7. nice 8. has
Down: sandwich

Exercise 3:
Sentence B is number 1. Sentence C is number 2.
Sentence A is number 3. Sentence E is number 4.
Sentence F is number 5. Sentence G is number 6.
Sentence H is number 7. Sentence D is number 8.

Exercise 4:
1. Thomas Tallis is a composer and an organist.
2. a) The ghost of Thomas Tallis must walk through the school at night because they don't play his music at 'his' school.
   b) –
3. Tom put the music on Terry's desk.

Exercise 5:
Tony is the farmer, Peter is the bus driver, James is the taxi driver, and Ben is the teacher.

Goodbye, Elephant!

Exercise 2:
In picture 1 it is 3 o'clock, and in picture 2 it is 4 o'clock. In picture 1 Elephant has got six tins on its tail, in picture 2 there are five tins. In picture 1 Elephant is catching a mouse (Tom), in picture 2 he is eating a chocolate mouse. In picture 1 there is a terrible noise, in picture 2 Elephant is eating. In picture 1 the other mice are excited, and in picture 2 they are happy.

Exercise 4:
1. Tom's ideas are: All the mice bark like a dog; tie ten tins to the cat's tail.
2. No, cats aren't *really* silly like this. This is a story about Tom, and he is the best mouse in the world!

Exercise 5:

a) A snake is going upstairs.
Four mice are looking at a piece of cheese.
A Mexican is riding his bike.

b) –

Tom's adventures in Catland

Exercise 1:

One cat is singing, two cats are playing the guitar, three cats are skateboarding, eight cats are playing basketball, one cat is milking a cow. There are four other cows, too, and four cats are playing with eleven little pigs, two cats are sitting/riding on a horse, seven cats are having a picnic.

Exercise 4:

1. The cats are scared of Barker because he is a very big dog.
2. They want to find some young cats. Young cats do not fall over when they see a big dog, and they know the exciting things in Catland.
3. Barker and Tom run to the stage. Barker barks, and Tom is sitting on Barker with a spear.
4. a) Yes, it is a good idea. Tom needs Barker to find Susie, and Barker is scary for cats. He is a big dog.
   b) –

Exercise 5:

cheese, (toy) dog, (toy) cow, (London) bus, football, game, apple, ruler, alarm clock, computer/PC, (toy) chicken, pencil, island, sofa, pizza, ship, cupboard, cake, (school)bag, (toy) Susie (mouse)